dear love

bianca perrie

For all the lovers of love.

III

Dear Love,

I found you.
And in these pages,
I will immortalize you.

Number One: On Meeting.

Let me start by saying:

I asked the universe for you.

When you arrived,

I expected you, and

I knew I was ready.

When you walked

through the door,

everything in me

stayed steady –

even though

I wanted to go

weak at the knees.

See,

that just wasn't me

anymore.

I was at ease.

With me. With love.

I understood.

When we met,

I understood.

Do you get it?

You would make good

on what I understood

about love.

There was no doubt.

No need for an out.

Call me general, like

this was my assignment.

The universe had come

into alignment.

I had asked it too.

Boldly,

egotistically.

And it did,

for –

You arrived

to a dinner party

in casual attire,

and still,

there was not

a doubt in my mind.

You arrived.

When we locked eyes,

I understood.

I was beyond believing in

love at first sight.

That was a folly of youth,

of inexperience.

Which I no longer was,

because of time...

Time halted.

Voices quieted.

A moment.

I've always

found something

mysteriously beautiful

about things that move

slowly:

The sunrise,

the sunset,

postal,

R&B music,

bubbles,

sloths,

a deep kiss.

Time.

So,

sometimes,

I try to picture moments

occurring in slow motion.

The moment I saw you

for the first time

was like that.

Time slowed.

For me.

For you.

Do you know why it slowed?

Do you get it yet?

Maybe not,

but I understood.

I knew how special you were.

From the tips of your hair

to the tips of your toes,

I knew.

You may have felt

as though you have

walked the earth

forever alone

and that no one

saw how exceptional you were—

I did.

I do.

When you said hello

for the first time,

it took my breath away.

You left me breathless,

do you get it?

The first time

you formed your mouth

to say my name,

my world imploded.

I floated on the sound.

Because I knew,

I had to know you.

What made you smile?

What brought tears

to your eyes?

What made your blood boil?

What got you high?

What, what, what.

And why, why, why?

I sought to know

everything about you

from the minute

you were born

and seek to know everything

for every minute

you're alive.

When it came time to sit,

we didn't adhere

to the seating chart.

We were lead by heart;

confined to a corner,

we did a la carte.

We sat side-by-side

when we ate,

dialoguing

between bites and plates.

It was easy.

Never giving any word

a second thought,

a bee to honey,

we were caught.

I was wrought

with questions.

You warmed to me,

You opened up to me,

as if eloquence

were your birth right.

I didn't want to

get ahead of myself

that night,

so I slowed.

The conversation,

and the moment.

You still didn't get it yet.

That was the only threat

about you.

Otherwise,

the second hand ticked,

clockwise,

just barely.

Unfairly,

this night ends.

As nights must.

With trust and lust,

we say goodbye

anyway.

Before we leave,

we make plans

for another eve.

Do you get it?

It's so easy.

Believe me,

this is it,

I know.

This isn't for show.

This is for real.

And I have chills,

thinking now

of how

I used to

recklessly roam –

and you look like a home,

and now,

I think of how,

I must have been,

marching through,

always on my way

to finding you.

Number Two: On Dating.

You told me

how you stressed

about where to take me.

You felt,

so much depends upon

the location of the first date.

Like you'd be saying

what you thought of me,

and you didn't want

to get this wrong.

You hadn't known me long,

despite whatever pace

I envision you,

you had to make a decision.

Your honesty

washes over me,

a refresh,

and I feel my attraction to you

in all that I am,

blood, bones, and flesh.

Our first date

was on a balcony

under a setting sun

and an eve's breeze.

You had on black ball shorts

and a white jersey.

I had on a long skirt

and a cropped tee.

I looked at you

and you looked at me.

We stood side to side

with such ease,

looking,

we found we had

a million things in common –

a love of books, art,

music, and autumn.

Our souls had clicked,

instant and tightly.

Rightly, so,

this connection seemed

beyond reality.

Our second date

was at a studio,

late at night,

under a white moon.

We both were wearing black,

from head to toe.

Both in skinny jeans,

looking like a fashion show.

Vinyl records lined red walls,

music to which

only we were attuned.

We listened,

and danced,

and sang,

and swayed,

a growing fondness

on display.

Our next date

was at a museum

in the middle

of the afternoon.

They call this phase,

a honeymoon.

You are the art

against a backdrop

of history and culture.

Of all the beauty

in this world,

you are unlike any other.

Surrounded by treasure,

relics, and festoons,

you're the thing

I could worship,

if it wasn't too soon.

Getting to know you,

getting to know me,

has been

(and will continue to be)

an endless adventure.

We are adventurers now.

Partners in a daring experience.

We wore many different hats

as adventurers.

In bucket hats,

we were archaeologists,

digging through our pasts,

sorting our memories,

healing our traumas.

We saw each other,

right to the bones —

no judgements,

no high horses,

no thrones,

and we began to wonder,

is this where we

can build a home?

In top hats,

we were historians,

researching people,

understanding places,

documenting dates.

You were you in person

and you were you on paper,

I knew I was in good trouble

as we moved acre by acre.

Curator, landscaper —

so many hats.

A crown.

That's a hat you wore too.

Easily.

Too easily.

Regally.

The era of regency,

you'd fit it so perfectly.

Witty,

well-mannered,

and marriage material —

You moved magisterial.

I could only call you regal.

I could only call you king.

Fairy tales are for children,

but I was once a child,

and so,

that conditioning

does not dissipate

so easily,

and so,

the concept of

happily ever after

is borne of fiction,

and so,

it's problematic,

but damn me

if I don't want it—

the castle and the happily ever after

with you.

But these words

stay trapped inside me,

oh, no,

let them go,

I can't.

It's too early.

Falling,

slowly, sure,

but surely,

in love with you.

Despite the fantasies

in my brain,

this would be a slow burn.

Without excess, without undress,

you continue to impress me.

We share an innocent kiss between us.

And yet,

it is an intimate soul's kiss.

If this is a sort of home,

well,

I could get used to this.

Number Three: On Travelling.

So, yeah,

we have a growing comfort.

A growing familiarity.

So yeah,

we think to test that.

To go away together.

To see how we cope

with the pressure –

of a new place,

a different language,

being confined to sharing

a tight space.

So, yeah,

we do this.

First up,

a weekend staycation.

We travelled

three hours

by train.

But before we boarded,

you asked

if I needed a snack,

and if I needed to use

the ladies room.

Blushing,

we made a quick stop

and then resumed.

You carried my luggage,

and you led the way,

I settled in

to this role

(a little too)

easily.

Your eyes were everywhere,

and you were on guard –

like in the Queen's yard,

a blood red outfit,

and a lofty black hat

in large,

as if it were your charge,

you wanted to protect me.

My usual sharpness dulled,

my desire

to seek out danger

dissolved,

like salt in water.

Dare I say,

I felt safe.

I trusted that

you were paying attention,

so that I didn't have too.

And I thought,

again,

of how easy this was.

Between our books and banter,

we arrived

in what felt like a beat,

a flash;

the express train had

made a mad dash.

We grabbed food

from the station,

sustenance for the walk

to the hotel,

we played silly

little question games,

but I'm convinced,

by now,

you knew me well.

And shortly after checking in,

our stomachs simultaneously began

stinging,

swirling—

Uh, oh –

we realized in sync –

Food poisoning.

If I wasn't too busy,

aching,

sweating,

sicking –

I'd have the decency to feel

the prickling

of embarrassment.

What a development;

this couldn't have gone less of

how it should've went.

We hardly left the room.

Despite the doom and gloom,

you kept our spirits up.

A joke,

a story,

a song or

a show.

And I

hadn't the heart

to mess

with your flow.

You stroked my back

when I needed it,

brought water

to my bedside,

pat away every single tear

when I cried.

I didn't have to pride or hide.

From this,

with quickness,

I bore witness,

in health,

yes,

but also in sickness.

Into reality,

you brought this notion—

There you go again…

moving in slow motion.

Next up,

an overseas holiday.

A longer one.

I can't recall how we decided,

perhaps a joke,

but one of those jokes

that was said

with a hint of honesty,

asserted audibly –

Paris.

And we do it all.

A Seine River cruise,

and Moulin rouge.

Escargot

served on a flower,

a trip up the Eiffel Tower,

Champs-Élysées

and Le Louvre,

I was consumed

by it all.

Paris had that

je ne sais pas.

We remained in awe.

We admired

We adored

Paris' tourist attractions

We admired

We adored

each other in action.

You didn't waste words,

saying things like beautiful –

Instead, you said,

Beguiling, incandescent, divine.

A once-in-a-lifetime.

You called me a triumph.

L'amour l'emporte.

Somehow, you stop short

of saying it too.

J't'aime, again, and again,

the words are in my brain.

The words are in my chest.

They are at the tongue of my tips,

but they die at my lips.

I now know

another way

to say I love you,

but I cannot say it yet.

I must move slow,

degree by degree,

for love

in this life

is a journey.

Voyager, c'est vivre,

and then we leave.

Behind us,

our Parisian buffet,

It's not true what they say –

you can

come home again.

Number Four: On Relationships.

When it became apparent

we weren't interested in

seeing other people,

it only made sense

to become official.

A president sworn in,

a law passed,

official.

Something binding,

something visible,

something constant.

Official.

As we moved toward this,

our conversations changed,

deepened,

like Sleeping Beauty's slumber,

and like her awakening

by true love's kiss,

we discussed this—

lovers, couples, relationships.

we decided

we should

have a good understanding of this,

of what it means to us

to be good partners.

We thought of Adam and Eve,

and how she was made

from his rib;

not to be glib,

but she was a part of him

and he was a part of her,

fitting, and unremitting,

forever.

We thought of Paris and Helena,

the face that

launched a thousand ships

and started a ten-year war,

this is the stuff that

only a person in love

would opt in for.

We thought of Romeo and Juliet,

who, granted,

were young and brash,

but what a decisive love,

that made them want to act.

We thought of

Cleopatra and Antony,

Napoleon and Josephine,

Orpheus and Eurydice,

Tristan and Isolde,

Lancelot and Guinevere,

Bonnie and Clyde,

Shah Jahan and Mumtaz Mahal,

Elizabeth Bennet and Mr. Darcy,

Jack Dawson and Rose—

Names,

We thought of so many names.

Names that almost felt wrong

to say without the other attached.

A coupling unmatched,

Of which we've only scratched

the surface.

We'll be that.

Eternal, immortal lovers I say.

But we are going to make them

look like child's play.

Every love story is epic

in its own way.

If I may,

because everyone who has

ever loved someone

is immortal and eternal.

Their impressions,

always in the heart of another.

It's all so romantic,

so unintentionally so,

but we both see love

as something

for the ages,

on stages

(that's all the world).

Regardless if they were fact

or if they were fiction,

what they were to each other

inspired generations:

To talk about love.

To dream about love.

To be in love.

We'll turn our stories into

these kinds of legends.

It'll be as if we were destined.

For a slice of a second,

I might understand,

what would possess a person,

to fall on their own sword.

Consequences ignored –

At the hands of love.

And if it were time,

I would call for you

with my last breath.

My last word

would be your name.

In an exclaim,

it's you.

My Immortal Beloved,

you're ever mine.

A squiggle,

and a straight line,

I co-sign.

As you stated

your intentions,

of your being mine,

and me being yours,

there were no questions,

only answers:

Yes, of course.

We promise each other

more than just

comfort and honesty,

we promise each other

sacrifice and sovereignty.

We promise each other

loyalty, security—

A place where peace increases.

A place to always come back too.

Two households,

both alike in dignity,

in your home,

is where I lay

this scene.

Only second to

what's really been,

the other kind of home,

internal, unseen.

Number Five: On Sex

The first time:

I stared at you

from the passenger seat

while you drove me home.

My heart seemed

too gigantic for my chest.

Your palm rested

on my thigh

but the heat

from your hands reached

so many other places.

My love was too big

for just my body.

It bursted out of me,

exuding need,

yes,

I needed to consummate

this love with you.

I needed to know your body.

Palpitation, liberation—

Your pleasure was

my greatest aspiration.

Did you like that?

Would you crave it?

Could it drive you

to your wits end?

Ascend, and

let me be the one

to bring you

to the brink,

pull you back,

then push you

over the edge.

Free fall.

Unleash

unto me.

Free fall.

Into love.

Free fall.

Into forever.

Manifest

this endeavour

with me.

Give me your heart.

You've got nothing

to lose.

Give me your heart.

Don't hide from me.

Give me your heart.

I will hold it,

more carefully

than anyone else will.

Don't ask me how

I know that,

I just do.

It is an energy,

a feeling,

a mark.

Let me hold your heart.

We came so close so

our souls entangled,

separation be damned.

Please, understand,

my need is desperately grand.

And, so,

you will be absorbed:

all of you,

murky past included,

into my soul.

Once you've penetrated my soul,

you will be met with

undying understanding

in these arms.

Once you are steady

in these arms,

you will know love

unlike any other

in these lips.

In these hands,

you will find home.

Reveal yourself to me.

You are safe.

You will know you are safe.

You will know you are home.

And if you are,

so am I.

It's in our hands, now.

I'm in your hands now.

You will know me

in a way most

never will.

Your love…

the way you love me…

it is pure and it is ecstasy.

Pure ecstasy.

Racy,

lacy,

but also,

necessity,

sentimentally.

We must do this again.

The second time:

I knew,

without a shadow

of a doubt,

that I wanted to share

all that I am

with you

for eternity.

And eternally

still wouldn't be

enough time

for all the times

I want to make love

to you.

Seeing you,

for real

seeing you,

buck naked,

seeing you,

bare,

is an occasion

worthy of celebration.

This cataclysmic event

solidifies our bond.

A chemical bond,

Like water, hydrogen, carbon.

a lasting attraction-like bond.

This first marks

the first of another

forever.

And forever,

through redundancy,

sounds like a cliché,

but I don't know

what else to say,

I'm forever, love.

This is all types of love.

This will be big love.

In big moments.

It will be small love.

In small moments.

It will be shape shifting love,

so that it can fit-

into-all-the-

cracks-and-crevices-

it-needs-too-

to-be-fitting-love.

Our love will fit,

like a tailored suit.

I fit you

and you fit me.

Forever type of love.

Third time:

We spent so much of the day

running out the clock together,

we moved as mirrors,

and we became so synchronous,

we became confident

in our skilfulness,

I knew when you were near,

because I got goose bumps,

because my chest thumped,

because hair rose at the

nape of my neck,

from apex to depths,

I shivered.

We combine

Everything –

bodies, worlds, homes.

We combine

what cannot be explained,

only experienced.

Number Six: On Fighting.

When we settled in

to each other,

when we allowed

the mask to slip,

allowed both faces to show,

Thalia and Melpomene,

too free,

we found ourselves

underprepared.

Everything else

had come so easy

to us,

we hadn't thought

to prepare for conflict.

We'd been on the same side

of every battle,

every contest,

every tussle,

and never lifted a muscle;

it just was.

But then—

I arrived late to dinner,

forgetting to dial,

and you smiled

a little too long

at the waitress.

Press,

digress,

yes,

it only got worse

from there.

Old habits – Mine—

Saying I'm fine.

Pacifying myself with wine.

Taking this as a sign.

Shutting off,

answering in scoffs,

writing us off.

Rolling eyes, and

private cries.

Picking you apart,

savage from sweetheart.

Old habits – Yours—

Walking out of doors,

measuring in scores,

Seeking solace in whor—

other people.

Staying out late,

spewing words with hate.

Overstaying in bed,

revealing a hot-head.

On opposing sides,

in every fight,

we became enemies,

butting heads

about who was right.

Superman V Luthor,

Batman V Joker,

Ariel V Ursula,

arch enemies.

The worst of the worst.

The worst of it is,

even in these moments,

you moved slowly,

slow motion,

to me.

These moments lasted

mere minutes,

though they felt like hours,

and these moments are there,

at any speed,

in my memories–

enemies.

Like tectonic plates vibrating...

but friction.

Earthquakes,

tsunamis,

eruptions.

Big blows,

little blows,

We doled.

Our lifeline—

ECG beeps slowing,

cracks in palms showing,

Breaking, deflating,

weighting, frustrating,

costing, exhausting—

too heavy to hold;

We had to learn

how to fight.

New habits – Mine—

I tell you when

you get close to my line.

I listen actively,

having the capacity

to hear you and disagree,

I disagree politely,

but I am all ears.

I don't hide my tears.

When I criticise,

it's the issue,

not you.

New habits – Yours—

You stay —

With me until it's sorted,

a problem thwarted.

With a patience as great

as time is long,

you don't say

right or wrong.

You stay —

on topic,

rhapsodic, neurotic.

Separating the forest

from the trees,

you try to see

my side.

Solutions poured out.

Like rain, post-drought.

These things will come to pass.

I assure you.

I cast my vote,

betting on us.

Cast,

like a spell.

Cast,

like I was meant to

heal your fractures.

Cast,

like it's the role

I was born to play.

The course of true love

never did run smooth.

A Shakespearean truth.

And after a million

micro fights,

we put the world

to rights.

Number Seven: On Family and Friends.

Except friends came first,

not that their opinion

held more weight

in this dominion,

but they were a trial run.

They were a jury

of sorts.

Of public opinion,

they held the courts.

We both knew we wanted

a network of support,

so the stakes were high.

From evil eyes,

we fortified,

and began.

Love is a series of

dangerous quests and adventures,

an Epic of Gilgamesh,

if my friends didn't

approve of you,

that was a sort of death.

We might search

for the secret of revival,

but like survival,

their detest

is a morality

we'd have to accept.

Of all my friends,

I only had two,

who could make me

reconsider you.

Except you were you,

you were charm and smarm,

dear and sincere,

whizzing and giving.

You were you –

at your absolute best,

and they never stood a chance.

Edward in the meadow,

they were dazzled by you,

as I was.

All that

unnecessary worry

released,

and done and dusted,

at least.

A necessary next step,

a means to an end,

it became time

to meet your friends.

Not even two seconds in,

they gave me hugs and vin.

Not even ten seconds later,

we found a great denominator –

laughter,

so much laughter,

thereafter,

we connected,

on many levels.

What a thrill it was

for others to confirm,

in no uncertain terms,

what we already knew,

how well we suited.

The scarier part,

in truth,

was what we left for last.

Time to meet our families—

future, present, past.

In two separate dinners,

we tried to

find common ground,

build burly bridges,

wave white flags,

but there was

so much apprehension,

so much tension,

at the mention of the future

we planned together.

A member of my tribe

with a gripe sniped

cruel questions at us.

A member of yours,

perfect whirly curls,

finger twirls in pearls,

a rumour swirls.

We fought for us,

pound for pound.

Day after day,

they slowly

came around.

From this,

we learned:

We must protect our home

at all costs.

Love is the only thing

that costs.

Whether it's kept

or it's lost,

it costs.

The price of forever

certainly isn't free,

but if it's meant to be,

we pay the fee:

Sacrifice –

is the price –

pay it once,

pay it twice,

pay it thrice,

pay it as many times

as need be,

call it a shopping spree,

I love you, and

you love me,

and at the end,

that's all there will be.

Our legacy.

We loved.

Some were supporting of,

Some were dismissive of,

Some were speaking of,

Some were hateful of;

the above.

Still,

we loved.

Number Eight: On Engagement.

I told you,

before the time came,

exactly what to do.

Make it small,

carry me to city hall.

You didn't listen

to any of it.

When the time came,

I thought

I wanted

everything

to stay the same…

we had been so good

for so long,

I didn't want to chance change.

I should've had more faith.

For when the time came,

you pulled up in a Wraith,

helped me in,

put me in a blindfold,

bold as ever,

you drove.

Under a darkened sky,

I hadn't the inkling of an idea.

Where we were going,

why we were going…

But we promised

each other adventure.

Still blindfolded,

you guided us past sounds –

the whoosh of automatic doors,

the ding of a receptionist's desk bell,

the click of elevator doors.

You held me,

like for dear life,

as an elevator glided upright.

When we stepped

out of the elevator,

I couldn't find my feet

and you whisked me –

and it was a wildly,

consumingly perfect moment,

because loving you

was always like this,

a kiss and a whisk.

Beneath my feet,

carpet turned to concrete,

then a gust of wind

rushed past me,

then silence.

Something in me quieted,

a tree fallen in the forest—

and an orchestra played,

a symphony of choruses.

You whispered in my ear.

Now.

I raised my hands,

pulling back the blinders,

the bright flash of a camera,

I jumped.

There must've been hundreds,

thousands of roses –

petals strewn,

bunches hung,

an arch arose.

You propose.

A queen's coronation.

A screaming proclamation.

A roaring declaration.

Of love.

Yes,

yes,

a thousand times yes.

I'm glad

you didn't listen

to me.

As you slid

a diamond carat

on me,

all our fingers trembled.

I shook my head in shock.

I gasped for breaths.

I cried from overwhelm.

I recalled…

I recalled how some religions believe

before we're born,

we choose our life's purpose,

but the moment we are born,

we forget this,

and we spend our ninety or so years

trying to recall that thing

we came here to do.

I imagined…

I used to imagine

what that moment of recollection

might be like.

How the universe would rejoice

at the recalling of that choice,

and how promises reconnected

would be a purpose protected.

We dashed back inside,

though I no longer

felt the cold,

and the gold trimmings

on the wall,

and the rich burgundy-green

colour palette –

Is this the building where we met?

We got off on the right floor

and it came back with a whoosh,

there was a time,

only three years prior,

when we were both single

and out to mingle.

The place we met.

The place we met

was full of family and friends,

and they shouted congrats

in their silly cone hats,

and they raised champagne flutes,

they were all in cahoots.

It is a queen's coronation.

A screaming proclamation.

A roaring declaration.

A toast.

Throughout the night,

we received much advice:

Marriage is a commitment.

Marriage is communication.

Marriage is comedy.

Marriage is curiosity.

Marriage is coitus.

We make eyes

at each other

across the room,

like the first night we met,

only now I know

what you're thinking –

we speak in paragraphs and chapters

with our eyes.

My love language

is your existence.

It is this home.

This home,

our homes in each other,

is spiritual,

yes,

but it's also contractual,

official.

Thorough and through,

I cannot wait

to marry you.

Number Nine: On Marriage.

I really shouldn't use

wedding and marriage

interchangeably,

not really,

but that day,

I did.

One is the start of the other.

The wedding.

That day

we were a union united.

Expedited,

though clear-sighted.

The wedding,

the climax.

After all the acts,

we came to our peak,

and standing on feet.

For the bride.

In my fluffy white dress,

and my final minute alone,

I processed:

the gravity of this thing.

Bound by word and ring,

from my dressing room,

I immersed,

thanking every atom

in the universe,

you are mine.

Today, then

for forever.

Fittingly,

we chose a castle

as the venue.

I know, I know,

ingénue.

I care not.

Not, knot.

That day,

we tied the knot:

The sky was a

robin egg blue,

a beautiful hue,

the clouds rolled,

the sun shone gold –

it was all backdrop,

miniscule matters,

props and flatters

for that day.

We chose the rose

as our decorative flower,

it had such power,

even overused,

it proved to be captivating,

clusters here and clusters there,

clusters in every colour.

Roses,

because you gave them to me

on occasions –

special ones,

silly ones,

insignificant ones –

it was the poetry in the gesture,

the power in the thought,

and the precision in the execution.

As I moved row by row,

floating in your direction.

Friends and family

directed their attention,

but my eyes were on you.

They didn't fall away,

no,

not at all.

Their celebration was our applause.

A standing ovation for our love.

On that day,

love

seemed too tiny a word,

too few letters

for what I felt.

It would have to be spelt

with gazillions of

characters to even compare.

I was there.

Welcome.

You looked at me

like I invented magic,

like I told the world to spin,

like I single-handedly

scattered the stars

across the sky.

And I,

I knew that look,

I knew you were seeing me

in slow motion.

You took my hand in yours

and squeezed three times,

our secret code,

our sign –

I love you.

It's too small for this moment.

But I'm convinced,

there isn't enough

paper,

ink,

or words

in the world

to express

what you are to me.

Vows we wrote together,

as read by the presenter:

I promise to always

see you as a poem.

Knowing you

yet knowing

there's much to know still,

containing the things

I need,

and the things

I didn't know I needed,

every word you hold sacred,

both simple and complicated,

both complete and in progress,

put together and a mess,

worthy of adoration,

a never-ending conversation,

a higher vibration,

a grand inspirer,

a life magnifier,

the object of my desire,

my soother of aches,

for goodness sakes,

my poem.

Do you take...

I do, I do, I do.

To the power of a zillion.

A vermillion kiss.

Poems may come,

and poems may go,

but look at Istanbul #2461,

mounted in a museum.

On display for all to see.

We will be persevered

in that way,

my honeysweet.

It's hard to say,

now,

when our forever began.

Because again,

that day felt like

another beginning.

Once upon a time...

Once in this lifetime,

I promised forever to you.

Promising forever to you

was the easiest thing I could do.

Then,

to actually do it...

Number Ten: On Home.

We are crumbs,

less,

sprinkles

in the grand scheme

of the universe's twinkles.

The chances of us

being alive

at the same time

in the history of everything.

The chances of our

paths crossing

given the number of

people on this planet.

And the chances of us

finding a love

like this

exists...

Microscopic—

nanoscopic…

So, why then?

How then?

Does it feel predestined

for us to be?

Every moment of

my life

before this,

every line

in every poem,

leading me to you,

leading me to home.

e.e. cummings taught me

No Thanks,

no gatekeepers shall

hasten my advance.

I'm almost there.

Almost there.

The word home

is a lot like

the word love,

four little letters, and

they could make beggars

of us all.

Things we yearn for.

Things we chase,

but I am home with you

and you are my place.

Our house of cards,

sturdy in the wind,

if I ever blow away,

I will be

called back,

Dickinson's epitaph,

well,

there's no place like home,

clicked Dorothy,

as she made her

illustrious plea,

leaving the grandiose behind,

returning for peace of mind–

there really is

no place like you.

So, make yourself at home

in me

as I do thee,

my sweet home

sweet home sweet,

home isn't just where the heart is,

it's where all the hearts are.

Love and home.

We can be a big home

or a small home,

a home in the country

or the city,

one that is made of brick

or of straw,

one that is flawless

or flawed–

it does not matter.

I am home.

With you.

In you.

In me.

In this life.

In the next.

In all of them.

Mayhem.

Chaos.

The beginning

and the end.

To comprehend,

too incomprehensible,

sometimes,

I confess,

I must take it

day by day.

As the sun sets,

I smile,

knowing

that I am loved

by you.

When the sun rises,

I smile,

knowing a new day

means a new chance

to show you,

you are loved by me.

You are my happy ending.

My ultimate truth.

I have metromania because of you,

my motivation, my muse.

You are the

epitome of this

collection of poems,

my poems

have been

my home,

now you are,

my poem and my home.

A mimicry to make Aristotle proud.

Poetics and Lovers,

that's my crowd.

To them, I vowed.

And to them, I bowed.

To the universe,

to meeting many demands,

thank you for new homelands,

and for these thoughtful hands,

blessing and praying,

let me end with that saying.

Signed,

Your love.

Fin.

ABOUT THE AUTHOR

Bianca Perrie was born in Toronto, Canada. She holds a Bachelor of Arts degree in English Literature and a Bachelor of Education degree. When she's not writing about love, she's reading romantic novels, watching romantic movies and/or binging any TV series with a will-they-won't-they couple. Her other faves include coffee, wine, chocolate, and puppies.

MORE BOOKS BY BIANCA PERRIE

Printed in Great Britain
by Amazon

84246282R00062